WHO IS RESPONSIBLE FOR THE FENTANYL CRISIS

By Peter Barski Pharm D

"A journalist can't hope to do much good unless he gets a good deal hated; that's the way he knows how his work goes on."   Henry James

AUTHOR'S NOTES

I coined the term "establishment" from the book A People's History Of The United States by Howard Zinn. In his book, the establishment is the collection of the US Government, the court system and big corporations, but for the purpose of this book, it is only inclusive of our government and court system, not the big corporations. "But wait, wasn't it the big drug manufacturers who helped start the opioid epidemic?" you might ask. To some extent, yes, but I am not discussing the opioid epidemic in this book, I am discussing the fentanyl crisis taking place in this country right now, and there is a difference. In fact, I had originally titled this book, "Is The US Government Responsible For The Fentanyl Crisis?" but as I progressed in the story, I realized that it was not just our government alone that started this disaster, it is also linked to the many pharmacy benefit managers (PBM's) as well. Of course the PBM's are part of the big corporations of this country, and one might thereby reason that establishment could thereby be inclusive of all three of Howard Zinn's definition of said word, but no, as you will read, other corporations have suffered billions of dollars in fines and even "big brother" oversight now by the government, thus necessitating the need to not include corporations into the word. This will all become clearer as you read into the book. One final note; it is not my intention to throw blame around regarding this subject. I would much rather find a solution to the problem, and I have dropped some ideas of how to do that along the way. But in order to solve any problem, one must first determine what started it, and so I have brought this book out into existence. Whether or not people will heed its advice is yet to be seen. I remain skeptical and hopeful at the same time.

INTRODUCTION

Imagine if you will having a beloved relative residing in an adult living facility (ALF). Perhaps it is your mother or grandmother. You chose a particular residence because of its stellar reputation for taking care of its clients. It was a decision not made lightly as your loved one is advanced in age and frail in nature. She had suffered a fall a few years back and fractured her hip. Given her age, the orthopedic doctor advised against her having surgery, but informed you that she could be kept comfortable on pain medication. So given her limited mobility and need for nursing care, you made the hard choice to count on a professional facility to provide residential nursing assistance for her.

So it came as a shock to you to hear from your loved one on the phone one day informing you that the facility was not able to give her the evening dose of pain medication last night, and because of that she was not able to sleep well. They had also failed to give her morning dose as well and she was in a most uncomfortable state physically because of this. You assured her that it must have been an oversight on the nursing staff and that you would call to find out what had happened.

After some shuffling around from the front desk to nurse manager to nursing desk, you finally reach someone who knows what is going on. The short of it is the pharmacy they use to supply your loved one's medication with did not have the medicine in stock, so the nurse could not provide her with anything for her pain. "Well, that is an easy fix," you think to yourself, and you suggest to the nurse to just have another pharmacy fill it. "Oh, but we can't as we are contracted with that pharmacy to provide our facility with all of our medications."

"But if the pharmacy is out of stock of something, then you should be able to just use another pharmacy," you reply.

"Yes, you would think, but we require all medications to be blister packed, and only a select few long term care pharmacies provide that service. The pharmacy did inform us that they will have the medicine back in stock next week."

Not satisfied with this explanation, you ask for the phone number of the pharmacy they use so you can find out why they are out of a common pain medication that your loved one needs for pain relief. After explaining the situation to a few people and being placed on hold for long periods of time, you finally reach a pharmacist on duty who is aware of the situation and knows what is going on. Observe the following conversation......

"Yes ma'am, we are currently out of Percocet, but we will have it back in stock on Monday, the first of the month."

"Well, why are you out of stock, is there a manufacturer backorder of that medication?"

"No ma'am, we have reached our allotted maximum amount of pain medication we can order for the month, but we will be able to order more on Monday, the beginning of the month."

"Well today is Friday, which means my mother will have to go without her pain medication for three more days."

"Yes ma'am, I'm sorry for the inconvenience."

"Perhaps you should raise your allotted amount per month so that this does not happen again."

"I wish it were that simple ma'am, but our wholesaler where we order our medications from mandates how much we can order per month."

"I'm sorry, but why on earth would they limit the amount of pain medicines you order each month, did your pharmacy do something wrong?"

"No ma'am, we are in good standing with both the wholesaler and the DEA."

"So wait, let me get this straight, even though my mother has a valid prescription for Percocet, written by a doctor in good standing with the state, you can not fill it because you have reached the maximum amount of pain medication you can order for the month?"

"Yes ma'am, that is exactly what I am saying."

"Well, how is it then that the drug wholesaler can dictate, or should I say restrict how much of any medication you order?"

"Oh, this sort of policy was implemented after the opioid epidemic, more specifically after they were sued by the DOJ."

"Okay, but what does that have to do with a long-term care pharmacy that fills prescriptions for nursing homes? It isn't like you are filling pain medicine for drug addicts."

"Well, it is a blanket policy covering all pharmacies in America, a one size fits all kind of thing if you will."

"Well obviously it isn't working that well."

Too hard to believe? Think again. I have worked in a long-term care (LTC) pharmacy before and saw this happen first hand. So why are these callous policies in place, and what were the events that led up to it? Why have millions of Americans switched from taking prescription pain medications to taking fentanyl sold on the street? How does all this affect a person who suffers a simple broken bone and is given a prescription for a pain medication by their emergency room doctor? What can be done to change things? Let us take a closer look and get to the bottom of this obviously broken situation.

THE OPIOID EPIDEMIC –
A BRIEF HISTORY

"Coke is …..dead as dead. Heroin's coming back in a big…..way." Pulp Fiction 1994

When did the opioid epidemic begin? The government would have you believe it was the fault of the Sackler family, the former owners of Purdue Pharma, known for the drug Oxycontin, but they are just "scapegoats." The truth is the American drug consumer was shifting away from cocaine to opiates way before Oxycontin became commercially available in 1996. Visionary film writer and director Quentin Tarantino mentions this fundamental shift in American taste for drugs in his 1994 blockbuster film Pulp Fiction. Why heck, the 160mg strength of Oxycontin did not become available until July of 2010. To put that into perspective, in the beginning of 2008, under pressure from the Food and Drug Agency (henceforth FDA), Methadone 40mg wafers were restricted from distribution and sales to retail pharmacies. "The 40mg strength is not FDA approved for use in the management of pain. Thus, the distribution and availability of the 40mg formulation will be limited to registrants in only those settings using the 40mg formulation for the appropriate indication." (deadiversion.usdoj.gov) What are those settings? Opioid detox or maintenance treatment of opioid addiction (methadone clinics). This is just one example of restrictions placed on drug makers and wholesalers by the FDA and DEA in the wake of the opioid crisis. This shows that the government saw the crisis evolving before Purdue Pharma became a "major player," so to speak. But when did the opioid epidemic start? It is hard to pinpoint, but to lay the burden of the blame on Purdue Pharma or the "villioness" Sackler family, as the press would have you believe, is just plain shortsighted. While it is true that the company's promotional practices of the drug Oxycontin to healthcare providers was in full overdrive by the late 1990's, can we lay the burden of the blame on them? Not anymore than we can for Budweiser advertising beer on television after a drunk driver causes the death of someone while being involved in a fatal car crash.

What is clear is that by the first decade of the 21st century, prescriptions for opioid medications had skyrocketed. It is difficult to obtain prescribing data from the 20th century, but it is said that by 2012 more than 255 million prescriptions were dispensed for opioids in the United States, with a dispensing rate of over 81 prescriptions per 100 persons (cdc.gov). That is a country in crisis mode. Clearly we had a problem, but how many of those prescriptions were actually written for Oxycontin specifically? Far less than the general public was led to believe. What was also available back then were drugs such as methadone, Vicodin (hydrocodone products), Percocet (oxycodone products), Opana (oxymorphone), Ultram (tramadol) and Roxicodone, which was available in a generic version (plain oxycodone immediate release tablets). This was much cheaper than Oxycontin at the time.

As a matter of fact, by mid 2010 Purdue Pharma had reformulated Oxycontin, making it difficult for people to crush and inject it. This deterrent formulation also kept people from snorting and smoking it as well. Meanwhile, the immediate release and generically available Roxicodone was and has remained in its original version, and in this author's opinion, a far more sought after product than Oxycontin. The fact that Purdue Pharma went to the effort of making Oxycontin abuse deterrent speaks volumes for the company. All the while you had other drug manufacturers like Mallinkrodt, Actavis and Abbott producing millions and millions of pills for the consuming public, not to mention the drug wholesalers who distributed those pills to the multitude of pharmacies that provided them to said public.

So who is to blame for this explosion in opiate use? Should it fall on the drug manufacturers, the wholesalers (Cardinal Health or McKesson), the pharmacies, or the doctors who prescribed them? The government, specifically the DEA and DOJ, have deemed all of the above as guilty, with lawsuits against some of the biggest companies coming down to billions of dollars, including the lawsuits against the Sackler family. We will address these lawsuits in more detail in a later chapter, but it is obvious that there was much blame to go around. One thing we do not hear about is the Center For Disease Control's (henceforth CDC) change on their guidelines for opiate prescribing back in the 1990's to reflect a more liberal practice of prescribing opiates to help treat a patient's pain. Not until after the opioid crisis became apparent did the CDC take a more conservative approach, recommending shorter days supply of opiate therapy for patients presenting with acute pain symptoms. Would it be unfair to say they had a role in the overprescribing of pain medications?

Whatever your opinion is, what is clear is that an already shifting "taste" from cocaine to heroin was being fueled on by an overzealous prescribing of opiates. Taking a Percocet after all was far more acceptable than shooting up heroin. Opiate use had also infiltrated the middle class with their insatiable appetite for spending on what they deemed "socially acceptable." Tack on the dark web with sales of illicit drugs hitting millions of dollars a year (ie Silkroad) and you had an all out frenzy. Obviously something had to be done, but would the actions of the government be beneficial or detrimental? Let us take a look at some of their actions to determine which it is.

ORDERING RATIOS

Nothing, and I mean nothing has done more to lower the amount of prescription pain medications from reaching the public than the implementation of ordering ratios. This may surprise a lot of people given all the media attention on major lawsuits against the big companies in the healthcare industry, and that will be looked at in a later chapter, but it is a simple fact. As of 2020 the dispensing rate for opiates was 43.3 prescriptions per 100 people. That is a significant drop from the numbers at the height of the opioid epidemic just some eight years prior. But at what cost has this decrease come? Before we consider that, let's briefly describe what ordering ratios are.

Back "in the day," so to speak, any pharmacy could order any amount of controlled or narcotic substances without limits or restrictions. The pharmacy profession after all is one of the most trusted professions in America, and up until the 21st century there never seemed to be a spotlight of shame on them. But the pharmacy business is just that, a business, and it is a consumer driven business at that. When demand for a certain consumer product rises, what does any business do? They carry more of that product. It may have been a long time coming, and left unchecked, the system implemented by the pharmacy business was bound to have some unscrupulous players, but in necessity the entire pharmaceutical industry was doing exactly as any consumer driven business would do, and that was to keep up with demand.

The government, being somewhat slow to catch on to this trend in opiate usage, began holding companies "accountable" for the surge in opiate usage in America. How did they do this? By suing the large corporations billions of dollars in fines, it created a ripple effect on the entire industry, with the most obvious being the implementation of ordering ratios. Although I cannot link the government directly to this policy, it only began after drug wholesalers like McKesson and Cardinal Health were sued by the DOJ. All the other smaller wholesalers soon followed suit, thereby restricting how many controlled substances can be ordered by the pharmacies that are contracted with them. This was a blanket policy covering all forms of pharmacy institutions: retail, hospital, compounding, long-term care, ect. If you intend to open a pharmacy, you have to specify what kind of pharmacy you are going to open and apply accordingly with that state's Board of Pharmacy (BOP). Obviously if you are operating a long-term care pharmacy, as was noted in the opening chapter of this book, your clientele are going to be much older than your average retail setting, so your needs will be different. Unfortunately the drug wholesalers in this country do not take that into account, casting a net of restrictions across the whole spectrum of pharmacy settings. After paying out billions of dollars in DOJ settlements, their main concern was to prevent that from happening again. Even if the smaller wholesalers were not fined by the DOJ, their actions have also followed the big company's lead.

So what are these ordering ratios? Essentially for the pharmacies ordering it means that they have to order a certain amount of non-controlled drugs before being able to order a controlled or narcotic substance. This can be a 3 to 1 ratio, 4 to 1 ratio or even higher. This is all kept track of by the drug wholesaler from which that pharmacy orders from. For the most part these ratios are in tablet count, so that if a pharmacy orders say one thousand lisinopril 10mg tablets (a non-controlled blood pressure medicine), then that qualifies them to order say 300 oxycodone tablets. This policy is used by the majority of drug wholesalers, with certain exceptions, which we will touch on shortly.

And if you are opening a new pharmacy, many wholesalers will not sell you a single controlled substance for six months, even though you have a valid pharmacy license from the state BOP and a valid DEA registration license. This license allows you to order controlled substances in the state you are operating in. By the way, if you are operating a pharmacy in the state of Florida, that license costs over $800 and has to be renewed every two years. So even though the DEA approves your business to purchase controlled drugs, wholesalers can still restrict your ordering them until they "establish a working relationship" with you. This limits your ability to provide proper patient care, at least for the first six months you are open. When establishing an account with a drug wholesaler, there is also now an exhaustive application process that a pharmacy owner must go through, including credit checks, but also a questionnaire asking such things as "which doctor in your local area prescribes the most controlled drugs," and "which controlled drugs are you dispensing." Is that fair for a drug wholesaler to do? Not in my opinion. One could say it is paranoia, but wholesalers will chalk it up to "due diligence," as a way for them to establish a client relationship with that pharmacy in order to determine their ordering habits. What this really does is limit that pharmacy from servicing their community, and ultimately eating away at that pharmacy owner's profits.

There are some drug wholesalers who mandate a dollar ratio, thereby further limiting how many controlled drugs a pharmacy can order. Take for example the 1000 count bottle of lisinopril 10mg I mentioned earlier. A good price for that stock bottle by any reputable wholesaler would be around $20. So with a drug wholesaler who uses a tablet ratio of say 3:1, a pharmacy can order three bottles of a 100-count oxycodone product, regardless of the price. But a wholesaler that uses a dollar per dollar ratio, that would limit a customer to just one bottle of a 100-count oxycodone product, for example Percocet 5/325mg tablets. The drug wholesalers who implement this policy are usually much smaller than a Cardinal Health or McKesson, but they will accept a new pharmacy client and sell them controlled drugs without a preliminary waiting period.

All of this never was an issue for pharmacists to deal with before. One can argue that this sets in place a system of checks and balances to help prevent another explosion of opiate drug usage in America, and they would be correct. But by throwing this net over all forms of pharmacies in practice, not just retail, it has caused undue suffering to certain people who shouldn't have to go without their pain medication. I touched on this in the introduction. Of course senior citizens are going to suffer from painful conditions much more than someone under the age of 55. Examples of these are arthritis, acute gout flare ups, shingles and fractures. Why should a long-term care pharmacy that services only nursing homes and adult living facilities (ALF's) be subject to ordering ratios? It's pure nonsense.

There is also another type of patient that should never have an issue receiving pain medicine, and that is a cancer patient. Can you imagine being diagnosed with terminal cancer at the age of forty, being prescribed Oxycontin to give you a baseline, long-acting opiate and Percocet for your breakthrough pain, and then not being able to find a pharmacy that will fill your medicine? Typical reasons a pharmacy would give this person would be: "we are not accepting new patients for pain medications right now;" "we are currently out of those medicines;" "those drugs are on a nation-wide backorder right now;" "since you are not on any other medications, we can't take you here at this pharmacy." Given the patient's age as well, pharmacy employees will be that much more inclined to think that this person was a drug seeker with no real need for such medications. There should be no reason why a patient diagnosed with cancer can not get any opiate medication prescribed by a doctor. If a patient is given a cancer diagnosis, and if that diagnosis code is written or typed onto the prescription, that person should be afforded the right to take that prescription to ANY pharmacy they so choose and get their medication filled. Why should they be restricted to using a chain pharmacy due to their insurance limiting them to using one? Unfortunately with the stigmatism and insurance restrictions in place right now, a cancer patient will most likely encounter these issues. Perhaps if drug wholesalers removed ordering ratio requirements for the subsection of cancer patients, they would have an easier time getting their prescriptions filled. Just an idea.

Going back to the topic of ordering ratios, there are "bad actors" on both sides of the equation: the pharmacies ordering the drugs and the wholesalers who distribute them. Take for example a pharmacy manager who wants to be able to order more controlled drugs because it is profitable for them to do so. Being an established customer with a wholesaler with a 3:1 tablet ordering ratio contract in place, they order three one thousand count bottles of the before mentioned lisinopril 10mg tablets for a total cost of $60. By doing so, they are now able to order three one hundred count bottles of immediate release oxycodone 30mg tablets. Now even if they never dispense any of the lisinopril, and it ends up expiring on their shelves and must be disposed of, it would still more than make up for that loss by what they can charge a customer filling oxycodone 30mg tablets without insurance. For example, by charging a cash patient $400 for 100 tablets of the oxycodone, they have more than made up for the loss incurred by ordering those unused lisinopril tablets. Why would a pharmacy charge so much for 100 tablets of oxycodone? We will get into that later.

On the other side of the equation are the drug wholesalers. The fact that they dictate which ratio they can implement is a powerful tool that can be wheeled about at their discretion. There are also the wholesalers who charge a whole lot more for an item than other distributors. For example, I have seen McKesson charge over $75 more for a generic version of the Epi-Pen 0.3mg than ParMed charged. They are able to do this because their controlled substance catalog is vastly wider than ParMed's, so a pharmacy is somewhat stuck with paying higher prices for many items due to their need to order controlled drugs from them. A prudent pharmacist could shop around different wholesalers, finding the best price on the medicine they are ordering, but that is a two-edged sword. By ordering medicines from multiple sources, they also lower their total amounts being ordered from their main wholesaler (ie McKesson), thus lowering the amount of controlled drugs they can order due to the ordering ratios put in place. You can be sure these larger wholesalers are aware of this, and yet it is a practice they can get away with because it appeases the DEA. The only thing the DEA cares about is controlling the outflow of opiates, and as long as that happens, they don't look into these company's pricing practices.

Another fact: Northstar Pharmaceuticals, a generic drug manufacturer, is the subsidiary of McKesson, the largest drug wholesaler in America. Also true is that Northstar is based out of India while McKesson's headquarters are in Texas. Another fact is that Northstar makes controlled and narcotic drugs as well as regular non-controlled medicines. That means that McKesson covers the whole spectrum of drug distribution: manufacturing, pricing and distributing. What I am curious about is what kind of governmental oversight is being incorporated when a drug wholesaler also has access to the drug making process. It is scary enough to think that a generic version of my blood pressure medicine is made and shipped over here all the way from India. I wonder if the containers these drugs are shipped over in are climate controlled. It is a whole different story as to how much money is being made by a company that makes, prices and distributes its own medicine.

"Well, thank goodness for my prescription insurance. I only have a $10 co-pay for generic medications, so I don't have to worry about all that," someone might say. And yes, to a person who is not taking opiate medications, that is a good thing. But let us look at how Pharmacy Benefit

Managers (PBM's henceforth) in conjunction with the restrictive ordering ratios implemented by drug wholesalers are having a negative effect on the pricing of opiate medications by retail pharmacies, which has ultimately led to the public seeking fentanyl products on the "street."

THE NEGATIVE EFFECTS OF PRESCRIPTION DRUG COVERAGE

A large percentage of Americans have health insurance, spurred on by the implementation of "Obama Care." Whether or not this was a good thing for the general public is not up to me to discuss, but with Obama Care came prescription coverage being offered to the vast public as well. Prescription drug coverage is also touted as a "benefit" by large employers and corporations to their employees, after they pass a "probationary period" of course. There is of course a large percentage of people who are self-employed or work for small companies that do not offer these benefits, so they often use prescription discount cards to help them save money on their medicine. An example of this would be GoodRx, which has gotten so popular now that it is a publicly traded company on the NASDAQ. But that is exactly my point, these Pharmacy Benefit Mangers (PBM's) and discount card providers are all "for profit" companies with one goal in mind, to make money. They do not care about saving you money as many people would think. So how does this all work, and what does it have to do with the fentanyl crisis? Let us start with prescription discount cards first and go from there.

If you are self-employed or uninsured, all you have to do is Google "free prescription discount cards" and you would have a plethora of options to choose from, with GoodRx being the top choice. Why wouldn't someone sign up for one, it would certainly save you money? Of course you have to "sign up" for them, which means you have to provide them with information. This includes your name and email address. If you want an actual card to carry in your wallet to present to the pharmacy, then you will have to give them your address as well. All of this goes without saying that whatever information you give them is sold to third party businesses. Thus comes the spam via email or through the post office. Tolerable? Perhaps to the person who just cares about lowering the cost of their medications. But that is not the only way these discount card companies make money.

When you present your discount card to the pharmacy staff, they need to add it into your "third party" or insurance section of your profile. It is added exactly as any other prescription card would be. To identify the card so that the claim can be processed electronically online, basic information on the card must be entered, again just as if it were any other regular insurance card. This will include a BIN number and PCN number. A member ID number specific to the cardholder will also be entered, and in some instances a group number as well.

The pharmacy staff member (technician or pharmacist) will then type up the prescription information and submit it to your discount card processor online, which will then approve or deny the claim. Reasons why the claim would be rejected are discussed further on in this chapter. When the claim is approved, it tells the pharmacy how much to charge that individual for that particular amount of medication being dispensed. A label and prescription receipt is then printed. What that customer does not realize is that each time that pharmacy submits a claim to the discount card provider, it is charged anywhere up to one dollar per transaction submitted. So if that customer has five different prescriptions to fill and the pharmacy submits all five claims online to the discount card carrier, that pharmacy will be charged upwards of five dollars. Not only that, but a drug that would have cost the patient say $10 cash price (out of pocket or no insurance) would now only cost that patient perhaps $2, thus lowering the gross profit for that pharmacy.

For the reader's information, GoodRx reported over $184 million in revenue for the quarter ending in December 2022. Big business indeed. Let us not forget that now that company has knowledge of every medication you take, how many you get and how often you fill it. Valuable information for a "for profit" business, allowing it to tailor what kind of advertisements you will receive.

So why would a pharmacy even accept any discount in the first place? The answer is easy: for increased foot traffic. Of course the general public is going to want to save money, so accepting a GoodRx card is good business, for the large company chain pharmacies at least. If your local Publix supermarket gets you into their store to fill your medicine, chances (or should I say odds) are excellent you will spend some money in the grocery store while you are waiting for your medicine to be filled. Have you ever noticed that every CVS and Walgreens pharmacy is located in the back of the store? That exposes the customer to all the items that store carries, thus increasing the likelihood that that customer will buy something while waiting for their medicine.

But for the small, independent pharmacies that carry a much smaller inventory of products outside of the pharmacy counter, the loss in gross profit incurred by accepting these cards is not worth it to them. Hence there is an increased movement of these pharmacies who outright refuse to accept discount cards. And can you blame them? It is not only because of the lower gross profits and fees charged to them that they are not accepting them, though that is good enough reason not to. That is especially pertinent when it comes to opiate medications. The fact that drug wholesalers have limited the amount of controlled substances a pharmacy can order (by means of ordering ratios discussed in the previous chapter) means that these drugs are not as easily available as they once were, thus creating a bit of a higher demand for them amongst the people who are still being prescribed them. Is a pharmacy manager going to charge a patient only $15.35 for ninety tablets of generic Percocet 10/325mg (GoodRX price for the south Florida area; last updated April 8, 2023) when they can charge over $100 to a cash customer? I don't think so, especially if that pharmacist can only order a few hundred tablets of Percocet every month due to ordering limitations. Can you see the dilemma now?

Sure, for a "big-box" corporate pharmacy filling over five hundred prescriptions a day, carrying enough Percocet tablets for their core customer base should not be a problem, but for that pharmacy that fills only fifty to a hundred scripts a day, like many smaller independent pharmacies, keeping Percocet in stock for the general public can be a daunting task. So of course these pharmacies are not going to accept discount cards; it makes no business sense at all. It essentially all goes back to supply and demand. If a desired product becomes less available, the price will go up.

Now let's look at PBM's and prescription drug coverage. Imagine now that you have worked for a big corporate company for a year and have passed their probationary period. You are now eligible for health, dental and prescription coverage under their plan. After waiting for your cards to arrive in the mail, you feel relieved to have health insurance and drug coverage. Then one day your sixteen year old son tears his rotator cuff while out skiing with some friends. You take him to the emergency room where he is treated and sent home with a Percocet prescription for his pain. You then proceed to your favorite locally owned independent pharmacy to get his prescription filled. The staff there are always friendly and it never takes long to get your prescriptions filled, unlike those big-box chain pharmacies that can take upwards of two hours just to fill one prescription. When you go inside and present his Percocet script, you advise them that you just got insurance and show them the card. You are told that unfortunately they don't accept insurance for that medication, but you can pay cash if you would like. You ask how much it would cost for the 21 tablets that were prescribed and are told $42 (two dollars a tablet). You hesitate for a moment, but then remember your son sitting in the car feeling uncomfortable from his injury. Not wanting to have to wait long for his medicine, you agree to pay it and in less than five minutes they have it filled and ready. "Worth it," you think to yourself in time and effort. But why wouldn't they fill it through your company's insurance plan?

Well as mentioned before, these PBMs are for profit companies, being insurance companies. For an insurance company to remain profitable, it must take in more money in fees than it pays out in claims. If an insurance company ends up paying out more than it brings in, it goes bankrupt, as we have seen in recent years with many homeowner insurance companies. But these PBMs are flourishing, I assure you. Besides taking in premium fees and processing fees to make money, these companies pay out as little as possible for the claims processed every time a prescription is filled. Being in the pharmacy business, I see first hand this issue each and every day. But before I give you some examples, let us identify who these PBMs are.

The most common, or biggest PBMs that most people are familiar with are Caremark (CRK), Blue Cross/Blue Shield (BCBS), Express Scripts (ESI), and Aetna. There are also your state medicaid cards that offer prescription coverage, but just like food stamps, only work in the state in which they were issued from. That means that if you cross state lines to visit family members and become in need of a prescription fill, you will have to pay out of pocket for it. There is also AARP for medicare aged citizens, and a handful of other carriers (ie Cigna).

An interesting fact: CVS pharmacy "merged" with Caremark in late 2006 which, according to the SEC, "provides for the combination of the two companies in a transaction structured as a merger of equals." Take a moment to think about that. The largest retail pharmacy company in the US with over 9,600 store locations and over $300 billion in revenue (2022) merges with the PBM Caremark. Sounds very similar to McKesson, the largest drug wholesaler, owning the drug manufacturer NorthStar Pharmaceuticals. But wait, it gets even better. Not only does CVS own Caremark, it owns Aetna, another PBM. And all of this has received the approval of the SEC. So what does this mean, besides the consolidation of businesses in a horizontal manner? Well, the most obvious thing, or should I say, the most pertinent, is that this company, CVS, which knows how much it is paying for it's medicines (its core business being retail pharmacy) now owns two major PBMs, which determine how much they will pay out for each prescription claim submitted to it. This not only includes CVS, but any retail pharmacy. What I want to know is if there is any oversight put in place to prevent CVS's PBMs from paying a pharmacy less money than it would a CVS. And that is if the patient can even get their prescription filled at their pharmacy of choice. Aetna and Caremark will many times restrict which pharmacies you can get your prescriptions filled at. So even though you may want to get your scripts filled at your local, independently owned pharmacy to avoid the headache of waiting two hours or longer at a CVS or other big-box chained pharmacy, you may not be able to. The claim could be rejected with a message stating you must use a CVS Pharmacy or pharmacy not contracted with provider. And if the medicine prescribed is a maintenance medication, meaning that you will need to stay on it for a long period of time, your PBM can mandate that you use their mail order pharmacy. Now you can call your PBM to complain about this, and they may even let you get it filled at your favorite pharmacy, but you will have to pay a much higher co-pay in order to fill it there. These PBMs do this in order to discourage their clients from using "out-of-network" pharmacies. The question is, is this legal? How can a Caremark mandate that you use a CVS pharmacy when that PBM is owned by CVS?

Now let us take a look at some practices these PBMs are doing to discourage your smaller sized pharmacies from wanting to accept them for controlled substances. Keep in mind that the sole purpose of these PBMs is to make money, so the less they pay out for a claim submitted to them, the better for the company. If they can get out of paying for a claim all together, even better.

For example, let's take insulin, which we can all agree on is very expensive, especially in the United States. When a customer gets their insulin filled at a pharmacy, they pay their copay and then go home, thinking that is the end of the matter, and for them it is, but for the pharmacy it is not. You see the PBM that processed the claim reserves the right to audit any and all claims submitted by the pharmacy for payment, at any time. Things that are always asked for in an audit are a copy of the prescription, ordering invoices from the pharmacy and a copy of the signature of whoever picked up the medication. Let's dive into all three of these items and see why they are always requested by a PBM during an audit, and whatsmore, how they find reasons why not to pay for the claim.

By examining a copy of the prescription, a PBM can ascertain that the pharmacy had a reason to fill the said medication and was not just randomly sending claims to the carrier for reimbursement on items they are not actually selling. Some PBMs will even mail their client a list of medications filled under their name each month and at what pharmacy it was filled at. Some may even call the client to verify that they actually had medication filled. This is all done to prevent fraudulent billing and unfortunately, is a necessity to prevent a few bad apples from profiting by false measures.

The other reason why PBMs ask for a copy of the prescription they are auditing is to determine whether or not the pharmacy filled it with the correct day's supply. You see, each prescription filled has to be submitted to the insurance (PBM) with the quantity filled and the number of days that quantity would last. It is a simple equation to compute when tablets are prescribed. For example, if a patient is prescribed ninety tablets of tramadol and they are taking one tablet three times a day, that would be a thirty day supply. Where it gets a little more difficult is when insulin, eye drops and creams are involved.

Insulin can be one of the most costly drugs to miscalculate the days supply on. Why, because if a pharmacy miscalculates the days supply on any prescription audited, the PBM will not pay the pharmacy for the drug dispensed, even though a valid prescription was on file. This goes for any drug, whether in tablet form or any other form. Since insulin is measured in units per milliliter (ml), and insulin vials come in various sized bottles (usually but not always 10ml's), and insulin pens are usually 3ml's in size, but in various concentrations, it can get very confusing determining the exact amount of days a prescription may last. Now one can argue that it is the pharmacist's job to make sure the day's supply is calculated correctly, and they would be correct, but ask that person if they have ever worked inside a busy retail pharmacy setting before and I can assure you that they have not. If they are a pharmacist working in some corporately owned pharmacy chain, I can almost guarantee that the pharmacy is going to be short staffed. Add to that the pressure of answering phone calls, patient counseling, immunizing patients, insurance rejections and the expectation of filling at least five hundred prescriptions in a ten hour day, that pharmacist is going to be hard pressed for time. Taking an extra few minutes to accurately calculate the day's supply on a new insulin prescription is a luxury many pharmacists just do not have. But let us say your friendly pharmacist working at your local independently owned pharmacy miscalculates the day's supply on an insulin prescription they fill and that prescription is audited by the customer's PBM. Perhaps they came up with a thirty day supply for a 10ml bottle of Novolog, when it was really supposed to be a 31 day supply instead. Let us also say there were twelve refills on the prescription so it would last the patient a whole year. Keep in mind that a PBM can request an audit on any prescription that pharmacy ran through them at any time, usually up to two years past the time the last claim for that prescription was filled, depending on that pharmacy's contract with them stipulates. Once that pharmacy sends a copy of the prescription to the PBM for review and it is determined that the day's supply was incorrect, even if by just one day, what do you suppose will happen? The PBM will get their money back is what, and not just for the first fill the patient received from that pharmacy, but also from all of the refills as well. Considering that one bottle of Humalog costs over $200, if a patient picks up one bottle a month, and the audit is performed nine months into the prescription's original fill date, we are talking about a $1,600 loss for that pharmacy. And what if that patient only picked up their Humalog once every 31 days instead of every 30 days, do you think that would make a difference? Absolutely not! The PBM would still take the money back from the pharmacy. Remember that the pharmacy has already paid for these vials of insulin when they purchased them from their drug wholesaler.

How does a PBM get their money back? Can a pharmacy just refuse to send them a check for the amount in question? Usually when a pharmacy signs a contract with a PBM so they can fill prescriptions for people in that network, they also must keep a bank account that both parties have access to. The pharmacy is also required to keep a minimum dollar amount in that account at all times. This obviously benefits only the PBM. If the pharmacy falls below that dollar amount at any time, they run the risk of being dropped by the PBM as a pharmacy provider. So what does all this have to do with the fentanyl crisis? We will progress to that shortly, lest I state the obvious that PBMs are really not a pharmacy's friend, they will look for any reason to not pay a claim. Given that controlled drugs such as oxycodone already have ordering limits for each pharmacy to adhere to, why would a smaller pharmacy take a chance at not being paid for a claim for that drug, let alone losing money on the claim, as will be discussed further on in this chapter.

As for requesting a copy of the pharmacy's invoices, the PBM is making sure that the pharmacy did actually purchase the drug being billed for. This is to keep a pharmacy "in check," so to speak. Again, there are "bad apples" out there that will bill an insurance plan for drugs that are not actually dispensed to the patient. But, the PBM has the power to deem an item not purchased in a timely manner or within a certain reasonable time period of the claim being processed. Let me give you an example. Say a drug wholesaler is running a special sale on Diclofenac 1% Gel. For one day only a pharmacy can save 25% on the normal cost of that drug, and if they order fifty or more tubes, they can get 50% off. Now most pharmacies would not use fifty tubes of Diclofenac 1% Gel in a week, and for a smaller independent pharmacy, fifty tubes could last them six months or longer. But saving 50% on that item makes good business sense, and they go ahead and order them to get the savings. Over the course of the next few months, they dispense the drug to various patients as per usual. Then one day they are hit with an audit by say Caremark, and this PBM asks to review all Diclofenac 1% Gel prescriptions that were billed over the last year. The pharmacy manager has to submit the invoice from earlier on in the year when he purchased the fifty tubes at a discounted price, but guess what, Caremark rejects payment on all of the Diclofenac 1% Gels he filled over the past several months because the medication was not purchased in a timely manner from when the claims were billed.

Finally, there is the signature log that is reviewed by the PBM to make sure the item billed for was actually picked up. Now some twenty-five years ago, back when I graduated from pharmacy school, people signed for their medicine on a paper log-book. The problem was storing all of those logs was cumbersome to say the least. They were bulky and required a lot of space. There were instances when boxes were disposed of by accident or even of a fire destroying them. Unfortunately for the pharmacy that could not produce a signature for the medication being reviewed by the PBM, they endured being docked payment for that particular claim. Today almost all pharmacies use some form of electronic signature pad to capture a patient's signature, but, if their system is hacked or wiped clean by accident, they would suffer loss of payment on any claims subjected by an audit. And remember, a PBM can go back as far as it likes to on a claim unless the contract specifies differently.

Let me give you a couple more examples of how the PBMs get out of paying claims to the pharmacy. Take for example the drug Monjaro. It is a very popular drug in the U.S. right now as it has shown to cause weight loss in patients using it. Pharmacies have been struggling to keep it in stock due to its popularity. Of course as with any new branded only drug, it is expensive. One box containing four injectable pens can cost a pharmacy almost $1,000. An issue with this drug is that as of the time of writing this book, the drug is not FDA approved for weight loss, so pharmacies that are filling the drug without a diagnosis code of diabetes on the prescription are subject to losing large amounts of money if they are audited. I personally have worked in an independent pharmacy that had a nurse practitioner working out of an office located in the back of the pharmacy. She often prescribed Monjaro to patients who were looking to lose weight, and the pharmacy filled quite a few of those prescriptions. Whenever the patient's copay was too high, the pharmacy would refer them to the Monjaro website where they could sign up for a copayment savings card. This card would lower each client's out of pocket expense down to just $25. Unfortunately for the pharmacy, the PBM that handled the claims for the Monjaro card audited them over all the claims submitted to that card. If there was no diagnosis code of diabetes on the prescription, the PBM refused to pay any claims that were submitted to it, costing that pharmacy thousands of dollars.

Another example of how PBMs get out of paying claims is to just not pay anything at all to the pharmacy filling the script. I am sure most of us are familiar with copays in relation to the medical field. You may have to pay a copay when you go see your doctor or get lab work done, and the same holds true for your prescriptions at the pharmacy. When you go to the doctor's office or to the pharmacy, your main concern is how much your copay is going to be. You don't worry about how much your insurance is paying your provider or pharmacy, that is between them and your insurance company. But what would you think if I told you that some PBMs will not pay anything at all towards the cost of the medication dispensed to you? Take for example Aetna insurance. I have seen a prescription of Dexmethylphenidate XR 40mg (generic Focalin XR) run through Aetna, which costs the pharmacy around $80 for thirty capsules, and they not pay anything on the claim. The only money the pharmacy got was the $15 the patient had to pay for their copay. So that one prescription cost the pharmacy a $65 loss. That is just for the drug alone, it does not take into consideration the business expenses for that pharmacy, which are payroll, software, hardware and rent. Also consider the fact that Dexmethylphenidate is a narcotic substance (class II amphetamine product), thereby being a substance subject to ordering limitations. Why would a smart business owner want to incur those kinds of losses on a product that they are limited ordering of? It makes absolutely no business sense whatsoever.

Many times if a PBM does pay towards a claim, the pharmacy still takes a loss on the prescription. Most pharmacy software systems will automatically show right away how much the pharmacy is making or losing once a claim has been adjudicated, and trust me, more and more claims are coming back negative these days. Nine dollars below cost here, thirteen dollars negative there. Out of say three hundred prescriptions filled in one typical day, there are usually twenty scripts that come back in the negative when run through a client's insurance. That is almost 10% of the total volume of prescriptions filled that end up costing the pharmacy to dispense instead of profiting from them. Put another way is that 10% of the prescriptions being filled through insurance aren't covering the cost of the medicine being dispensed. No wonder it is so difficult for a patient to find a pharmacy to fill their controlled drugs through their insurance plan. Why take a loss on a drug that is highly restricted now in aspects of ordering it and that is in such high demand? It makes no sense. So people are left to pay exuberant prices for these drugs in order to get them filled. Can you see why so many people are turning to the much more powerful drug fentanyl, which is so much more readily available on the streets, rather than incurring the costs of a doctor's visit and paying out of pocket for their meds? Now one might argue that there are thousands of pharmacies to choose from, and that there should be no problem getting pain medication filled if only the person would look hard enough. Well I assure you it is much more difficult than you think. Your chances of getting them filled at a big chain pharmacy are even less likely. Let us dive into the next chapter to find out why!

THE DOJS ROLE
(SHOW ME THE MONEY)

Guess how much the government has fined CVS due to the opioid epidemic. How about Walgreens or Walmart. How much money was collected from the Sackler family or McKesson, the largest drug wholesaler in the country? I should make a list, for the numbers are staggering. I'll start with the Sackler family only because of the inflated astigmatism associated with them.

Purdue Pharma/Sackler family: $6 Billion

CVS/Walgreens: a combined $10.7 Billion

Walmart: $3.1 Billion

McKesson: $7.4 Billion

Cardinal Health: $6 Billion

Mallinckrodt: $230 Million

Eli Lilly: $1.4 Billion

Overall the total amount of settlements from the pharmaceutical industry has topped over $50 billion. Let that dollar amount sink in for a minute. And there are more lawsuits pending as the DOJ announced in March 2023 of filing a complaint against RiteAid in relation to the opioid crisis. This is a company that is already teetering on the brink of bankruptcy, so leave it to the government to push them over the edge. Perhaps Walgreens or CVS will swoop in and buy RiteAid out, two companies that have already been sued by the government and are far more likely to follow the establishment's lead on wanting to stem the flow of pain medication to the public. What am I implying? Try getting your pain medication filled at one of these pharmacies and see how "seamless" it is.

In any case, states are "required" to spend 85% of their settlement funds on opioid remediation, with 70% of that allocated to future remediation. Remediation, what a word, but what does that mean exactly? The Oxford definition of it is: the act of remedying something. It sounds like a good way for states and government agencies to sit on much needed funds while they hash out exactly how to spend it. To me, a good way to fix the opiate problem is to provide free rehab services to people addicted to opiates, including their medications used to prevent withdrawals, ie Subutex and/or Suboxone. Is that being offered by your state?

What is clear is that the government wants the funds used, in contrast to when only 3% of the billions of dollars were used in the 1998 tobacco settlement. What I want to know is who is overseeing the spending of all this money? Where is the accountability? Even Judge Polster who presided over some of the massive settlements expressed his concern over the control and management of such large amounts of money.

The main point being, other than what all this money collected should be spent on, is with such fines levied against these big companies, they are bound to take an overly cautious approach to the purchasing and distributing of opiate medications. And to be certain, that is exactly what has happened, all the way from the major wholesalers to the big chain pharmacies. This has just put multiple barriers for people to face when trying to get their pain medications filled. Is it any wonder the general public has drifted away from the safer but harder to get prescription opioids to the now more readily available and much cheaper fentanyl out on the streets? All this to say that the government has now found itself caught with its pants down, not realizing that its actions have led to a new epidemic.

Getting back to the companies that have been negatively affected by these massive settlements, let's start first with the drug wholesalers. Now although I have not been able to find any specific mandate by the government, all drug wholesalers have now implemented ordering ratios. As long as a pharmacy orders enough non-controlled medications, they are able to purchase controlled drugs, but now on a much smaller proportion than before this whole crisis took place. If a pharmacy tries to order any controlled drugs over and above their allotted amount, that pharmacy is "red flagged." If a pharmacy red flags too often within a certain time period, the wholesaler can terminate their contract with them and report that pharmacy to the DEA. Wholesalers are now reporting to the DEA a list of the top ten pharmacies that order the most controlled substances in their state. All this to say that the drug wholesalers seem to be working hand in glove with the DEA.

Some things that the DEA does not mandate the drug wholesalers to do? Preventing a new pharmacy client from purchasing any controlled drugs for a set period of time. Forcing a pharmacy client to answer a questionnaire about local prescribing habits, with questions like "which controlled drug do you dispense the most of, name of the doctor who writes for the most controlled drugs in your area, and do you fill out of area prescriptions written for controlled drugs. Another thing the DEA does not mandate is the practice of decreasing the amount of controlled drugs a pharmacy can order when renewing that pharmacy's contract. Or how about increasing the required ordering ratio when renewing a pharmacy's contract. All of these requirements make it more difficult for a pharmacy, especially a locally owned independent pharmacy, to order and keep in stock opiate pain medications. Wholesalers justify these practices as being prudent, but in actuality they are just building up failsafe measures against being sued by the government again. If they can show the DOJ that they have taken productive measures in lowering the amount of opiate medications being distributed out, it shields them from punitive actions against them in the future.

We can see this kind of "cautious" measure being implemented at the retail pharmacy level as well. Just ask someone who may have herniated two disks in their lower back and have been prescribed pain medication by their back doctor. Perhaps they are in their early forties and are given a choice between invasive back surgery or long term opiate treatment to help alleviate their pain. They can not afford the back surgery and certainly can not take off six months from work to recuperate after said surgery. So the doctor prescribes them 120 tablets of oxycodone 10mg to be taken four times a day and Ibuprofen 800mg to be taken three times a day. I guarantee you that every CVS, Walgreens and

Walmart pharmacy in town will turn that patient away with any of the following excuses: "I'm sorry, we don't stock that medication here," or "that medication is on backorder," (which would be untrue), or "we are not accepting new patients for that drug right now."

Why would this person have such a hard time getting a legitimate prescription filled at these pharmacies? Because these companies have been sued for billions of dollars, and now company policy dictates that they can no longer fill opiate prescriptions indiscriminately. Even though this person is in need of immediate pain relief and presents these pharmacies with a legitimate prescription written by a doctor in good standing in the state, they will be shunned away time after time. Did the government see this coming? Their main concern was to lower the amount of opiates being dispensed to the general public; mission accomplished! Did the government see that the general public has now switched over to the more easily accessible Fentanyl on the streets? Apparently not.

I had to laugh when I read about the DEA removing prescribing restrictions on Suboxone and Subutex effective in June 2023. (www.inquirer.com/health/opioid-addiction). A too little too late move by them if you ask me. Too little because it really does not solve anything except for allowing any doctor with a DEA prescribing license to be able to write for buprenorphine products. Before this, a doctor had to apply for a waiver application in order to prescribe these drugs. They also had a limit on the number of patients they could prescribe these drugs to, thus limiting a person's access to these doctors who were eligible to write for these drugs. So yes, now any doctor with a valid DEA prescribing license can write for these drugs, but if you really want to impress me, offer their writing services for free. Better yet, have every state in America offer these drugs for free. That's right, let's take some of those billions of dollars the government has sitting around right now and provide these medications at no charge to those who are actively seeking help for their opiate addiction. And why we are at it, let's pay for people's rehab stays as well. There is a wise use of all that money. And if the DEA was serious in trying to control the fentanyl crisis, they would lift the controlled status on all buprenorphine products completely. They were able to change the controlled status of all hydrocodone products from a Class-III to a Class-II. So what was once a drug such as Vicodin or Norco could be written for a one month's supply with five additional refills, now has it limited to requiring a new prescription for each fill. So why not lift the controlled status on all buprenorphine products, thus allowing patients easier access to these medications? As it stands now, these drugs, being Class-III products, are subjected to the same ordering ratios as previously discussed, limiting how much a pharmacy can order. Shouldn't we make these kinds of drugs more accessible to the general public given the current state of affairs? An interesting tidbit is that a controlled drug prescription like buprenorphine automatically expires six months from the day the prescription was written, but a narcotic prescription has no expiration (on the federal level). That means that if you had a prescription for Percocet written say some two years ago, you can still legally get that script filled, whereas with a Subutex prescription would no longer be valid. How much sense does that make?

A main problem for people in recovery from opiate addiction is the cost of getting their prescriptions filled. Many people rebuilding their lives do not have health insurance, so they have to pay out of pocket for not only their doctor's visit, but also their medications. Just another headache to deal with for someone trying to get off opiate drugs, as if they don't have enough to stress over already. Of course if all states used their opiate settlement funds to pay for these expenses, this wouldn't be an issue, so show me the money!

According to a recent bipartisan report, overdose deaths cost the U.S. one trillion dollars annually (abcnews.go.com). This is based on the increase in overdose deaths encountered since 2018. Of course this can be blamed on the fentanyl tablets being smuggled up from Mexico which are currently flooding our streets, but I submit to you that our government left the public with no other choice but to use these drugs. By essentially eliminating access to FDA approved pain medications, which are of course extremely addictive, but are free of any adulterated substances, the Mexican cartel has stepped in to fill the void of supply. And they are making a lot of money doing so. Do you think these cartels care that hundreds of thousands of their customers in the U.S. are dying by using their product? Well, if they are deeply rooted in their culture, probably not. Just read about the atrocities committed by the U.S. during the Mexican-American War and reflect for a while about it. One thing is for sure, the DEA is not winning this war. Only a drastic change in thought is going to help us get past this crisis.

CHANGING THE NEGATIVITY ASSOCIATED WITH OPIOID USE

If you were able to sit in on a class of pharmacy students at any of our universities, you would be bound to hear a lecture or two about the perils of opiate medications. Perhaps you would hear something along the lines of "pain drugs are addictive and any prescription written for more than a six day supply should be heavily scrutinized, or "if I were you, I would not take a chance and fill medications like that." The schools now are producing pharmacists that are becoming increasingly hesitant to fill any such medications. They are taught to fear the DEA and that any visit from a DEA agent to their pharmacy spells doom for the pharmacist.

I'm sorry, but why don't these pharmacists just **do their job?** If a board certified doctor who has a valid DEA license deems it necessary to prescribe a patient an opiate medication, it's not a pharmacist's place to question it. If a doctor is unprofessionally prescribing too many pain medications to the public, it is the DEA's responsibility to handle that, not the pharmacists. We are not the "gatekeepers" as some boards of pharmacy may have you believe. It is their responsibility to make sure a controlled prescription is valid, but nowhere is it stipulated that a pharmacist should deny filling a prescription just because they are afraid of the drug being dispensed. That is just hindering a patient's access to medical treatment. Pharmacists can not just pick and choose which medicines they are comfortable filling. It just doesn't work that way. It makes as much sense as if a bartender refuses to serve a customer a Long Island Iced Tea because they felt it would get the customer drunk too quickly.

Perhaps you have seen on the news the story about a pharmacist who refused to fill prescriptions for birth control because of their religious views. But what if a teenage girl gets pregnant because her pharmacist would not fill her birth control pills? Yet six states allow pharmacists to deny patients of their medicine due to any moral objection they may have. My opinion both as a pharmacist and a Christian is for that person to either find a new line of work, or practice in a pharmacy niche setting where their moral beliefs will not interfere with their job.

If the DEA and pharmacy schools and boards of pharmacy are instilling that kind of fear into our future workforce, it is going to make the fentanyl crisis linger even longer. Let us just do our job and let the DEA do theirs. It is the job of the DEA to weed out those doctors that have questionable writing practices, not the pharmacists. Pharmacists need to stop being so narrow minded and selective when it comes to their work. And yet patients will hear all kinds of excuses for why they can't get their pain medicine filled. "We don't have that in stock at the moment." "That drug is on backorder." "We don't carry that medicine here." "We can't get hold of that drug at the moment." "I don't have enough of it to fill your prescription." Excuse after excuse.

It is a shame what lengths pharmacists will go through to not fill pain medications. It is getting so bad that many Americans are having to live in constant pain, pain bad enough to warrant a prescription from their doctor. The stigma associated with opioid use is shameful, even in the pharmacy profession. Many health care providers will never know what it is like to have to deal with Crohn's Disease, or ulcerative colitis, or rheumatoid arthritis or herniated disks. And even when a pharmacist has no qualms over filling these prescriptions, company policy prohibits them from doing so. Of course this can be attributed to the multi-billion dollar lawsuits our government was so quick to hammer down.

There was a time when a person was prescribed something by their doctor and had no problem filling their medicine. No excuses were given, no judgemental looks by the pharmacy staff. I mean do I really have to say it? Not all people taking pain medication are "junkies." Unfortunately I have worked with other staff members in the past who flung this term around every time they saw a prescription for an opiate medication. It's narrow minded.

Then there are the DEA agents who go around harassing pharmacies that are suspected of filling too many opiate drugs. They show up during regular business hours, unannounced and flashing their shiny badges, asking to see dispensing records, inventory logs and current drug inventories. And yes, there are a few bad apples in the pharmacy business, but on the whole, this is just a scare tactic to help curve the dispensing of controlled drugs.

I would like to take a minute to discuss the topic of addiction and all of the negativity that goes along with it. Obviously America is dealing with a crisis unlike any we have seen before. We can argue back and forth all day about the causes of this and who is to blame, but that isn't going to solve anything. It's time for our leaders to make prudent decisions to help solve the problem.

As for addiction, it is not just a homeless person's problem. Yes, a large percentage of homeless people are addicted to drugs, but they also have unmet psychological needs as well, something in the medical field known as a dual-diagnosis. But the truth is addiction affects all walks of people: millionaires, professional athletes, politicians and even healthcare providers. Anyone can become addicted to drugs. It is foolish to believe that addiction is a "poor man's" problem, but addiction can certainly make a person poor. I have seen people spend their very last dollar on drugs with absolutely no concern for how they were going to eat food.

Can we stop addiction completely in our society? Of course not, but we can start heading in the right direction. We can try to be more open minded and less impatient with people. Think more progressively. Accepting the fact that addiction is a disease state and not a character flaw is a good start. Perhaps looking at other countries to see how they are handling addiction might help. Learning how to reach out to a person struggling with addiction would be beneficial. Dropping the word "junkie" from our vocabulary wouldn't hurt either. Believing in second chances is essential, especially when dealing with someone in recovery. They need that kind of acceptance in order to overcome and succeed. By making any step in a person's recovery difficult or stressful, we impede the process. Another words, what can we do to make the recovery process easier? Most people in the early stages of recovery are exhausted, having neglected their eating and sleeping habits. They may have even hit a "rock bottom" of sorts, losing their jobs, homes and family. Everyone close to them may have lost their patience with them. An understanding of this is vital when offering recovery services to those in need.

Our country needs to add more drug addiction therapists and social workers to our workforce. More drug addiction psychiatrists would also be needed as well. People working on the streets to access their cities' needs are important, as are more affordable rehabilitation services. Let's get the government to get off their hands and become more proactive in a meaningful way. Perhaps sharing this book with your congressman may help. We can all do our part.

WHERE ARE WE HEADING NOW?

"Nothing like regular amphetamine use to make
you appreciate how dumb a lot of normal, non-
medicated human experience is."

-former CEO of Alameda Research Caroline Ellison

Like the legendary filmmaker Quentin Tarantino
boldly predicted in his movie Pulp Fiction, I also
am going to make a prediction about the drug
taste of the American populace. It seems that
now people are veering away from opiates and
moving to Adderall and amphetamines. It is not
uncommon for a typical pharmacy to get over ten
calls a day asking if they have Adderall in stock.
Most pharmacies I work in now in the retail sector
fill more Adderall prescriptions than opiate drugs,
which is a vast turnaround from just a few years

back. Even looking at your local sheriff's office website these days to see what people are being booked for will show more people being arrested for amphetamine possession versus fentanyl.

Many reasons can be given for this quick turn in American taste for drugs. One is of course the great difficulty in obtaining pain medications from their local pharmacy and the cost associated with it. Another is that boomers are far more reluctant to purchase street drugs from SnapChat than say a Generation Z would. The not knowing exactly what they are getting inside of a pill scares the crap out of most older people. Could there be lethal levels of fentanyl inside of their score, who knows exactly? Then there are the videos on YouTube of the streets of Kensington, with video bloggers filming people looking like zombies, standing in broad daylight for all the world to see. Add to that the horrors of people losing body parts due to necrosis of the skin from "tranq," and it is downright horrifying. Another reason, and this is just my opinion, is that Americans are just now waking up to the fact that they need to get back to work. The whole Covid-19 pandemic kind of put the workforce on pause for a while, with many companies laying off workers and smaller businesses shuttering up. Many younger people felt disposable, and rightly so. They were very reluctant to rejoin the workforce once America reopened. Only by the actions of the establishment, and by this I mean the federal reserve acting in conjunction with big business, allowing inflation to hit almost double digits and by the raising of interest rates to almost record levels, have the younger folks been pushed back into the workforce. Reluctantly so I might add. They feel lethargic and disinterested. Why put forth an effort when the company they used to work for previously found them so easy to let go of? They are bored and need some motivation. Enter amphetamine. Now the federal reserve (Jerome Powell) would have the public believe that this inflation is the cause of our big government writing all those "massive" checks to the public, but the truth is that they flooded the market with trillions of dollars to help keep stocks afloat during the pandemic. So the idea that the general public had so much extra money to throw around which led to the extreme inflation we are currently seeing, is laughable. In reality, the only people they were really helping were big companies, not Mr J.Q. Public, but alas, I digress.

During the pandemic, telehealth became acceptable in the medical community, and so did the prescribing of drugs from telehealth doctors. This helped usher in Adderall use as it became much more prescribed for than in the past. But this time, the big chain pharmacies have taken a far more cautious approach. Most if not all CVS and Walgreens pharmacies will now not fill any amphetamine products for a person over eighteen years of age. This has left the American consumer scrambling to find their Adderall, so much so that a major news broadcaster errantly did a segment on the "Adderall shortage" on their February 16th, 2023 nightly edition. This was a mistake, as there was no Adderall shortage; all the major wholesalers in the country had the drug in stock. What the news failed to report was that the big chain pharmacies were not filling these prescriptions for certain aged individuals, thus creating what seemed like a shortage, but really it was not.

Walmart has stopped filling Adderall prescriptions from telehealth doctors. Back when the Covid-19 pandemic was in full effect here in the U.S., the US Department of Health and Human Services (HHS) authorized providers to prescribe controlled substances via telehealth, without the need for an in-person medical visit (https://telehealth.hhs.gov). Now obviously this was implemented to help prevent the spread of the Covid virus, but some organizations found it to be an opportunity. Telehealth startups began to spring up offering patients an easy way to get controlled medications prescribed to them. Since all pharmacies are now set up to accept electronic prescriptions, this was an easy transition, and no person to person interaction was required. In fact, if the person's pharmacy offered delivery, that person did not even need to leave their home in order to get their medication. Very convenient indeed. And which controlled substance was being sought out for the most? Adderall, which became the most widely prescribed controlled substance through telehealth channels.

Of course the DOJ has been swift to investigate some of these telehealth companies, the most famous of these being Cerebral. Because of this investigation, Cerebral has stopped prescribing controlled substances to new patients. And so with these investigations by the DOJ and the big-chain pharmacies reluctance to fill Adderall, the smaller independent pharmacies are now carrying the load so to speak. Again, why would these smaller pharmacies want their profits slashed by filling this popular drug through insurance or discount cards? And of course now when one searches their local sheriff's office arrest records, they can see an increase in arrests for methamphetamine possession. And so it goes, the cycle of drug use in America, and where we are heading now.

CLOSING THOUGHTS

"When the necessity of a thing is generally felt,
they usually manage to accomplish it; but they
seem to feel pretty comfortable about waiting
till then." Henry James

For all their actions, the DEA, DOJ, and the
FDA have accomplished tangible results, if you are
only looking at the numbers. With the decrease in
the number of opiate medications being dispensed
now, one could argue their efforts were a success,
but our country has seen a skyrocketed increase
in the use of street drugs like fentanyl. The
backlash has been enormous because of this. It
is now costing our country billions of dollars to
manage this fentanyl crisis we are in. Something

different needs to be done, now. Let's stop trying to find blame and taking disciplinary actions against companies in the pharmacy field and start working together to find a solution to the problem. Forward thinking is required. The question now is, can the establishment come up to the task?

www.ingramcontent.com/pod-product-compliance
Lightning Source LLC
Chambersburg PA
CBHW060333130626
46553CB00003B/1005